My Parting Gift

Albert F. Chestone

Writers Club Press
San Jose New York Lincoln Shanghai

My Parting Gift

Published by Writers Club Press
an imprint of iUniverse.com, Inc.

For information address:
iUniverse.com, Inc.
620 North 48th Street
Suite 201
Lincoln, NE 68504-3467
www.iuniverse.com

ISBN: 0-595-00688-4

Printed in the United States of America

I dedicate this book to the beautiful and unforgettable memories
of my deceased wife Marcie Chestone
and the deceased husband of my present wife, Robert J. Ryan

Also to our adult children:

Lynn and Bill Null
Sue and Simon Ruebens
Thomas Chestone
Randy and Val Chestone
Cathy Chestone

Kathie and Brian Connolly
Rob and Lori Ryan
Nancy and Dave Romansky
Maureen Ryan

To my sister and brothers for their continuing support in preparing this book:

Mary Martino
Phyliss Chestone
Lou Chestone
Henry Chestone
Roy Chestone

And to my lovely wife Lorraine whose patience and encouragement
were a source of inspiration to complete this book

TABLE OF CONTENTS

PROLOGUE

Everyday I love you more and more...
Today more than yesterday and less than tomorrow.
I will not mind the wrinkles of your face.
My love will be deeper and more serene.
Think of all the springs which will fill our hearts.
My own memories will also be yours.
These common memories will entwine us more
And constantly between us other ties will interlace.
It is true that we will be old, weakened by age.
For as you know, I love you more and more;
Today more than yesterday and less than tomorrow.

Edmund Rostand

"MY PARTING GIFT"

My Dear One:

You have been my friend as well as my beloved.

It is this which I remember as I sit here, alone, thinking of you, worrying that indeed, we will not grow old together at all. One of us will precede the other to an awayness that I cannot, in my moment's solitude, comprehend.

You above all know how organized I am, or organized in my own scatty way perhaps?

I am going to surprise you. This particular time, this perhaps, most important moment of our lives together, I have come together with superlative organization.

And this because I love you. And it is because I love you that I have prepared for the eventuality of our not growing old together.

This book itself is my parting gift, created itself by a former widower, father of five. It is meant to be a guide for you to use in the coming days, weeks, years following my first flush of absence. Keep it as a reference guide. It contains all of the necessary forms to deal with your immediate needs as I am no longer next to you. If it is possible for me to think of you as you read this passage, as you thumb through this book, perhaps distraught, perhaps enraged, perhaps just deadly still, I think of you. And please, forgive me for those days I seemed to love you less than I do right now.

With passionate love and respect,

_____

_____
(date)

LOCATION OF IMPORTANT DOCUMENTS

Name of Document	Where Located
Last Will _____	_____
"Living" Will _____	_____
Birth Certificates _____	_____
Death Certificates _____	_____
Insurance Policies _____	_____
Immunization/Medical Papers _____	_____
Military Discharge _____	_____
Passports _____	_____
Valuables _____	_____
House Deed _____	_____
Past Federal, State, & Local Tax Matters: ____	_____
_____	_____
_____	_____
Burial Plot Information _____	_____
Motor Vehicle Drivers Lic.# _____	_____
Exp. Date Drivers Lic: _____	_____
Voter Registration Record _____	_____
Documents For Additional Vehicles Etc.: ___	_____
_____	_____

MY PERSONAL DIRECTIVE
PRIOR TO MY DEATH

LIVING WILL
(EXPLANATION)

A living will is a written declaration wherein you direct that certain life-sustaining treatments be initiated, withheld or withdrawn in the event you become mentally incapacitated and your condition is terminal or if you are in a coma with no hope of recovery.

LIVING WILL DECLARATION

To all those concerned with my health, my doctors, and my family, I, being of sound mind, do hereby request that this directive be followed in the event I become unable to participate in decisions regarding medical treatments in my behalf.

In the event, it becomes necessary to sustain or prolong my life, with no hope for recovery, by a mechanical apparatus, a tube feeding device or any other method, I do hereby request that the medical authorities refrain from using any such means to keep me alive.

My Personal Signature   (Date)

ADVANCE DIRECTIVE
(PRIOR TO DEATH)

POWER OF ATTORNEY

In the event, I am unable to communicate my medical decisions as to the utilization or continuation of *Life Support System*, I hereby leave this decision up to:

❏ My Family
❏ My Physician
❏ Hospital
❏ Other

_____

_____

_____

_____

My Personal Signature   (Date)

ORGAN   DONATIONS

DIRECTIVE AFTER MY DEATH
ANATOMICAL GIFTS

I have appropriately initialed the specified section of this statement.

Upon my death I wish to make the following anatomical gift:

1.   ___   Any needed body parts or organs.
2.   ___   Only the following specified organ or body parts.
3.   ___   Any transplant
4.   ___   Medical research
5.   ___   For a specific person, institution, etc.....

_____

_____ _____

_____

6.   ___   I **DO NOT** wish to make an anatomical gift upon my death.

_____

My Personal Signature   (Date)

WHAT YOU MUST DO FIRST

Things you must do immediately after I die, depending on the place of death and circumstances: (See check list on following page)

1. Contact family members.

2. Telephone police (if necessary).

3. Telephone family doctor (if unaware of death).

4. Make available any and all documents pertaining to anatomical gifts.

5. Contact funeral home (see check list)

6. Contact church (see check list).

7. Notify appropriate relatives and friends (see prepared list).

8. Obituary (see outline).

9. Immediate notifications (see prepared list).

10. Contact friends (see prepared list).

NAMES OF CHILDREN, STEPCHILDREN, GRANDCHILDREN

Names: First & Married	Address	Phones
Children		
		(Area code)
		(Area code)
		(Area code)
		(Area code)
		(Area code)
		(Area code)
		(Area code)
		(Area code)
		(Area code)
		(Area code)
		(Area code)
		(Area code)
		(Area code)

NAMES OF CHILDREN, STEPCHILDREN, GRANDCHILDREN

Names: First & Married	Address	Phones
Children		
		(Area code)
		(Area code)
		(Area code)
		(Area code)
		(Area code)
		(Area code)
		(Area code)
Step Children (if applicable)		
		(Area code)
		(Area code)
		(Area code)
		(Area code)
		(Area code)
		(Area code)

LIVING FAMILY RELATIVES, PARENTS, BROTHERS, SISTERS
AS OF _____

First/Last Names	Relationship	Residence	Phone #
			(Area code)
			(Area code)
			(Area code)
			(Area code)
			(Area code)
			(Area code)
			(Area code)
			(Area code)
			(Area code)
			(Area code)
			(Area code)
			(Area code)
			(Area code)

LIVING FAMILY RELATIVES, PARENTS, BROTHERS, SISTERS AS OF _____

First/Last Names	Relationship	Residence	Phone #
			(Area code)
			(Area code)
			(Area code)
			(Area code)
			(Area code)
			(Area code)
			(Area code)
			(Area code)
			(Area code)
			(Area code)
			(Area code)
			(Area code)
			(Area code)

GENERAL CHECKLIST
AS OF _____
(Date)

Local Police Dept.: _____ Phone #: _____

Hospital: _____
Name: _____
Address: _____
Phone #: (   ) _____

Personal Attorney: _____
Address: _____
Phone #: _____

Family Doctor: _____
Phone #: (   ) _____

Funeral Home: _____
Address: _____
Phone #: (   ) _____

Church/Temple: _____
Address: _____
Phone #: (   ) _____
Contact: _____

Type of Burial: Example, Earth etc... _____

Location of Cemetery Plot: _____
Name: _____
Address: _____
Plot/Site #: _____

Miscellaneous Service Arrangements: _____
Readings: _____
Music: _____
Pallbearers (to be selected by family): _____
Special Instructions (if any): _____
_____
_____

FOR OBITUARY

Name: _____ Date of Death: _____

Place & Date of Birth: _____

_____

Formerly resided in: _____

Biographical Sketch (include occupation, volunteer work, activities/clubs, schooling, honors, etc.):

_____

_____

_____

_____

_____

_____

_____

_____

_____

_____

_____

_____

_____

_____

BIOGRAPHICAL SKETCH
FOR OBITUARY (Cont'd)

Notify:

Primary Organization or Society:

Name _____

Address: _____

Phone: _____ Fax: _____

Notify Newspapers: (Usually handled by funeral home)

(Local) Name: _____

Address: _____

(Local) Name: _____

Address: _____

(Out-of-Town) Name: _____

Address: _____

Optional request at tail of obituary:

Please feel free to send donation to my favorite charity in lieu of flowers.

SPECIFIC AND IMMEDIATE NOTIFICATIONS

My beloved, please take a moment in order to make the following telephone calls without delay, as I have listed below:

For record purposes, and subsequent financial assistance:

"FEDERAL"   OFFICE OF PERSONNEL MGMT. (OPM)

(Employee)   Phone: 202-606-0133 or 888-767-6738

               Primary   Society: _____

                              Phone#: _____

               Primary   Organization: _____

                              Phone#: _____

                              Company Last Empl'd: _____

                              Phone#: _____

"NON-FEDERAL"   Company Last Empl'd: _____

(Employee)   Phone#: _____

               Primary   Organization: _____

                              Phone#: _____

NOTE: Be prepared to furnish them all the necessary personal facts they many ask for concerning me, as noted on the following page, titled *"Some Personal Facts"*. In the event a follow-up letter is requested including certain documents, refer to the sample letter set-forth in this book.

SOME PERSONAL FACTS

Print Full Name: _____

Date of Birth: _____

Place of Birth: _____

Social Security #: _____

Civil Service #: _____

Medicare #: _____

Personal Insurance Policies #: _____

Veterans Administration Claim #: _____

National Service Life Insurance #: _____

Armed Services Serial #: _____

Other: _____

_____

Current or Last Employer: _____

Dates of this Employment: _____

Current Marital Status as of /   /

Married: _____   Separated: _____

Divorced _____   Widowed: _____

Wife's Maiden Name (if applicable): _____

(if applicable) Wife's Name by Prior Marriage: _____

Prior Marital Status (if applicable): _____

Name of Deceased Wife: _____

Date of Death: _____

Name of Wife from whom Divorced or Separated: Name: _____

Date of Divorce: _____

Date of Separation: _____

Residence if known: _____

Other comments: _____

_____

FRIENDS

Close friends to be notified in the event of my death:
(in addition to my children, stepchildren, parents, brothers, sisters & grandchildren):

Names	Address (If Necessary)	Phones #'s
		(Area code)
		(Area code)
		(Area code)
		(Area code)
		(Area code)
		(Area code)
		(Area code)
		(Area code)
		(Area code)
		(Area code)
		(Area code)
		(Area code)

FRIENDS

Close friends to be notified in the event of my death:
(in addition to my children, stepchildren, parents, brothers, sisters & grandchildren):

Names	Address (If Necessary)	Phones #'s
		(Area code)
		(Area code)
		(Area code)
		(Area code)
		(Area code)
		(Area code)
		(Area code)
		(Area code)
		(Area code)
		(Area code)
		(Area code)
		(Area code)
		(Area code)

IMMEDIATE DEATH NOTIFICATION
OF A FORMER FEDERAL OR NON-FEDERAL EMPLOYEE
WHO WAS A MEMBER OF A SPECIFIC ORGANIZATION
FROM WHICH BENEFITS MIGHT BE DUE
(SAMPLE)

TO:
Society of Former Special Agents of the FBI, Inc.
P. O. Box 1027
Quantico, VA 2211134-1027

This is to advise you of the death of the individual listed below.

Name of deceased _____

Residence at time of death _____

Date of Death _____ Date of Birth _____

Member of Society? _____ Name of Chapter _____

FBI Service - From _____ To _____

Has Chapter Family Assistance Committee been notified? _____

If deceased not a Society member, name and relationship to member:

_____

Does survivor desire to receive *the Grapevine*? _____

If deceased had life insurance coverage through the Society, send appropriate claim forms to below-noted beneficiary.

Beneficiary _____

Relationship to Deceased _____

Residence of Beneficiary _____

Group Policy Number _____ Certificate Number _____

Please furnish the undersigned with claim forms for available benefits, if any, at the address below.

Sincerely,

_____
(Signature)

_____
(Type or print name)

_____
(Type or print address)

IMMEDIATE DEATH NOTIFICATION (CONT'D)
(SPECIFIC ORGANIZATION)
FROM WHICH BENEFITS MIGHT BE DUE YOU
(SAMPLE)

TO:

_____

_____

_____

RE: Death of Member

I regret to inform you that _____
                                                (Name of Decedent)
passed away on_____ .

Please inform me whether he/she was covered by a life insurance plan or had any other survivor benefits through his membership in your organization.

If so, please advise what documents are necessary file a claim by his beneficiary(s).

Sincerely,

_____
(Signature)

_____
(Type or print name)

_____
(Relationship to deceased)

_____
(Type or print address)

(Send "Certified Mail - Return Receipt Requested")

AS TIME PERMITS

As you grow stronger in my absence you may find some free moments to prepare specific correspondence for your immediate and future needs.

I have assembled some personal facts that may be helpful in the preparation of future correspondence regarding financial benefits to which you are entitled. I have also gathered for your assistance, helpful information concerning my personal assets, finances, insurance, medical benefits etc.....

AS TIME PERMITS, you may wish to review the sample letters I have prepared in this book which relate to benefits that are due you.

I AM A MEMBER OF THE FOLLOWING ORGANIZATIONS
(AND UNIONS IF APPLICABLE)

Name: _____

Address: _____

Title: _____

Name: _____

Address: _____

Title: _____

Name: _____

Address: _____

Title: _____

Name: _____

Address: _____

Title: _____

Name: _____

Address: _____

Title: _____

Name: _____

Address: _____

Title: _____

Name: _____

Address: _____

Title: _____

I AM A MEMBER OF THE FOLLOWING ORGANIZATIONS (AND UNIONS IF APPLICABLE) CONT'D

Name: _____

Address: _____

Title: _____

Name: _____

Address: _____

Title: _____

Name: _____

Address: _____

Title: _____

Name: _____

Address: _____

Title: _____

Name: _____

Address: _____

Title: _____

Name: _____

Address: _____

Title: _____

Name: _____

Address: _____

Title: _____

LICENSE AND DESCRIPTION OF ALL
LAND-SEA-AIR MOTORIZED VEHICLES
REGISTERED IN MY NAME

My Auto Driver's License #: _____

State Of: _____

My Auto Driver's License #: _____

State Of: _____

My Auto Driver's License #: _____
State Of: _____

My License # Of Other Motorized Vehicles: _____

Specify Vehicles: _____

License #: _____

Specify Vehicles: _____

License #: _____

Specify Vehicles: _____

License #: _____

Specify Vehicles: _____

License #: _____

TYPE & DESCRIPTION OF ALL OF MY MOTORIZED VEHICLES:
(CAR, TRUCK, TRAILER, MOTORCYCLE, AIRPLANE, ALL WATER VEHICLES)

TYPE	PLATE	MAKE	MODEL	COLOR	WHERE LOCATED

MISCELLANEOUS (COMMENTS):

_____

_____

_____

_____

PERSONAL FINANCIAL INFORMATION

Name of Bank: _____ Contact: _____

Address: _____

Phone: _____

      (Area Code)

In Name Of: _____

Personal Checking Account #: _____

Savings Account #: _____

Business Checking Account #: _____

Other Accounts #: _____

If Applicable: _____

Joint Savings Account #: _____

Joint Personal Checking Account _____

Additional Information _____

_____

_____

Credit Card Name (Visa, Master, Am. Exp. .etc.)	Card Number	In Name Of (Bank, Co. Etc.)	Exp. Dt Phone #
	( )		( )
	( )		( )
	( )		( )
	( )		( )
	( )		( )
	( )		( )
	( )		( )
	( )		( )

MY PERSONAL ASSETS

Real Estate owned by Me:

Description, Location, Lot, & Block:

_____
_____
_____
_____
_____
_____
_____
_____
_____

Jointly Held Assets: Explanation:

_____
_____
_____
_____
_____
_____

Information Concerning Assets Such As Vehicles, Boats, Etc.:

_____
_____
_____
_____
_____
_____
_____
_____
_____

ADDITIONAL PERSONAL ASSETS (CONT'D)

Description:

_____

_____

_____

_____

_____

_____

_____

_____

_____

_____

_____

_____

_____

_____

_____

_____

_____

_____

_____

_____

_____

_____

_____

_____

_____

_____

_____

_____

MY PERSONAL ASSETS SUCH AS STOCKS/BONDS/SECURITIES

Name and Address of Broker/Agency: _____

Address: _____

Phone #: _____

Personal Contact: _____

Concerning: _____

Name and Address of Broker/Agency: _____

Address: _____

Phone #: _____

Personal Contact: _____

Concerning: _____

Name and Address of Broker/Agency: _____

Address: _____

Phone #: _____

Personal Contact: _____

Concerning: _____

Name and Address of Broker/Agency: _____

Address: _____

Phone #: _____

Personal Contact: _____

Concerning: _____

Name and Address of Broker/Agency: _____

Address: _____

Phone #: _____

Personal Contact: _____

Concerning: _____

INSURANCE INFORMATION
LIFE/AUTO/HOME/MEDICAL ETC.

NAME OF INSURANCE CO.	ADDRESS	AMOUNT AND TYPE OF INS.	BENEFI-
CIARY			
1.			
2.			
3.			
4.			
5.			
6.			
7.			
8.			

Comments: _____

_____

_____

_____

ADDITIONAL PERSONAL FINANCIAL INFORMATION

ADDITIONAL PERSONAL FINANCIAL INFORMATION

DETAILED EXPLANATION OF MY:

1.   INSURANCE POLICIES
2.   PENSION PLAN COVERAGE
3.   MEDICAL BENEFITS
4.   OTHER

_____

_____

_____

_____

_____

_____

_____

_____

_____

_____

_____

_____

_____

_____

_____

_____

_____

_____

_____

_____

_____

_____

_____

_____

_____

_____

DETAILED EXPLANATION OF MY: (CONT'D)

1. INSURANCE POLICIES
2. PENSION PLAN COVERAGE
3. MEDICAL BENEFITS
4. OTHER

_____

_____

_____

_____

_____

_____

_____

_____

_____

_____

_____

_____

_____

_____

_____

_____

_____

_____

_____

_____

_____

_____

_____

_____

_____

PROCEDURE
FOR
CLAIMING BENEFITS

BENEFITS DUE AND PAYABLE TO YOU FROM:

1. NAME: _____

   ADDRESS: _____

2. NAME: _____

   ADDRESS: _____

3. NAME: _____

   ADDRESS: _____

4. NAME: _____

   ADDRESS: _____

5. NAME: _____

   ADDRESS: _____

Miscellaneous Comments:

If you wish to remain on their mailing lists, you must so advise them.

_____

_____

_____

_____

_____

_____

A LOVING REMINDER

Following my death, there are some additional telephone calls that will be necessary for you to make, or letters that you may have to prepare concerning benefits due you.

You will also have to make telephone calls or prepare letters to certain government agencies; companies or organizations, informing them of my death, in order to collect benefits that may be due you. In certain instances you will have to make available specific documents to the requesting company or agency.

In this connection, I have prepared sample letters for you to copy, which contain all of the pertinent facts that will be requested of you. The mailing instructions have been set-out.

EXPLANATION OF SAMPLE LETTERS

Specific samples of letters that must be written by survivor or family members, administrators and/or others to collect all benefits due.

The sample letters are to be used as a guide by the living spouse, and/or if applicable, next of kin, life partner, administrators or others.

These letters reflect specific explanations as to purpose, documents and mailing instruction.

"ALWAYS PREPARE DUPLICATES OF LETTERS BEING MAILED"

FIRMS AND/OR AGENCIES TO BE CONTACTED

The following pages reflect sample letters of the complete and exact name(s) of firms, and/or agencies from whom you are to receive benefits.

This list reflects the names and addresses of the various firms, government agencies, insurance companies, organizations, etc., (where applicable) to whom you will mail letters, as well as properly identified documents that maybe requested, as a result of your initial telephone call.

As an example: Survivors of Federal Civil Service Retirees: when applying for death benefits would correspond with:

Office of Personnel Management
Retirement Operations Center
Boyers, PA 16017

And Others As Noted Below:

1. NAME: _____

   ADDRESS: _____

2. NAME: _____

   ADDRESS: _____

3. NAME: _____

   ADDRESS: _____

4. NAME: _____

   ADDRESS: _____

5. NAME: _____

   ADDRESS: _____

6. NAME: _____

   ADDRESS: _____

7. NAME: _____

   ADDRESS:

SAMPLE NOTIFICATION LETTER - (FEDERAL EMPLOYEE)

To: From:
Office of Personnel Management
Retirement Operations Center
P. O. Box 45
Boyers, PA 16017-0045   Date:

Subject: ❏ Death of Federal Annuitant   *OPM-Pion#(if known)*
         ❏ Death of the spouse of a Federal Annuitant
         ❏ Death of Survivor Annuitant

Name of Deceased: _____
CSA/SCSF#: _____
Social Security Number_____
Military Serial #_____
Date of Death:_____

My relationship to the deceased: ❏ Spouse, (or)
❏ Relative (specify) _____
❏ Other (specify: funeral home, friend, etc. _____

If Spouse, Social Security Number: _____
Date of Birth: _____
I request the following change in enrollment in the Federal Employees Health Benefits (FEHB):
❏ Change from "Self & Family" to "Self Only"
❏ Continue "Self & Family" enrollment as deceased is survived by eligible dependents

Death Certificate: ❏ is enclosed   ❏ will be included with claims

Please furnish the undersigned with an application for death benefits, as well as a death benefits
Insurance Claim Form (FEGLI) Federal Employees' Group Life Insurance Programs.

NAME _____
PHONE & FAX #'s: _____
Best time to call: _____
Address _____

NOTE: For Annuitant Express Information Call 1-800-409-6528 For general inquiries, please
call the Retirement Information Office (202) 606-0500, Monday - Friday 7:30 am - 5:30 pm
Eastern Standard Time.

SAMPLE LETTER - TO EMPLOYER OF DECEASED
(FEDERAL & NON FEDERAL)

TO: FROM:

_____   _____

_____   _____

_____   _____

_____   _____

_____   _____

RE: Death of Employee

I regret to inform you that _____
                                            (Name of Decedent)
passed away on_____ .

It would be greatly appreciated if you could inform me of any benefits that might be due his beneficiaries, such as group life insurance coverage, pension funds, any accrued vacation of sick pay, terminal pay allowance, rewards, unpaid compensation, disability pay, balance in credit union, death benefits, or any other information that might be of value to the beneficiaries.

Please send me a list of any required documents and the forms necessary to claim any amounts due the beneficiaries.

                                       Sincerely,

                                       _____
                                       (Signature)

                                       _____
                                       (Type or print name)

                                       _____
                                       (Relationship to deceased)

                                       _____
                                       (Type or print address)

(Send "Certified Mail - Return Receipt Requested")

SAMPLE LETTER - TO EMPLOYER OF DECEASED
(FEDERAL & NON FEDERAL)
(SEE NEXT PAGE)

Many retirees are Veterans of the U.S. Armed Forces and a number of survivor benefits are available to the spouse and children of a deceased Veteran. Included in these benefits are:

1. Dependency and Indemnity Compensation (DIC). This compensation is paid monthly by the Veterans Administration (VA) to survivors of those who have died of service-connected disease or injury.

2. Death Pension. Payable o low-income widows and children of wartime Veterans who have died of causes not related to their millitary service

3. Funeral expenses. The VA will pay part of many Veterans' funeral expenses, including an allowance for interment or burial plot. Most funeral directors will assist in filing application with the VA for such allowance.

4. National Service Life Insurance (NSLI). If decedent was covered under this program, the following papers are needed to file a claim:

    a. Certified copy of Death Certificate.

    b. Certified copy of spouse's Birth Certificate

Survivors' benefits are not paid automatically and claim must normally be filed with VA within two years of the Veteran's death. For information or help in applying for Veterans' benefits, write, call or visit a Veterans benefit counselor at the nearest VA regional office, or VA hospital, listed in the telephone directory under U. S. Government. If there is no listing in your area, call the nationwide toll-free number, 1-800-827-1000

Families filing for insurance benefits should send request to the VA Regional Office & Insurance Center, P. O. Box 8079, Philadelphia, PA 19101

Note: A booklet entitled: "Federal Benefits For Veterans and Dependents" (S/N 051-000-002059) can be purchased for $3.25 from the superintendent of documents, P. O. Box 371954, Pittsburgh, 15250-7954, make check payable to: Superintendent of Documents, or an order may be placed by phone: 202-512-1800, using VISA or Mastercard. Fax order: 202-512-2250 with complete name and address, phone # (area code) VISA, or Mastercard # and Expiration Date.

Order Processing Code: 7589

SAMPLE LETTER TO VETERANS ADMINISTRATION

TO: FROM:

_____   _____

_____   _____

_____   _____

_____   _____

_____   DATE: _____

RE: _____
          (Full name of deceased)

The above-named individual passed away on_____. I would like to meet with one of your representatives concerning any benefits due his/her survivors. Listed below is what information I possess concerning the deceased. I will have with me a Certified copy of the Death Certificate and the Insurance policy. If any additional information is needed please advise me.

MILITARY SERVICE NUMBER _____ VA CLAIM NUMBER _____

NATIONAL LIFE INSURANCE NUMBER _____

BRANCH OF SERVICE _____
                                 (Army, Navy, etc.)

PERIOD OF SERVICE: From: _____   To _____

                                  Sincerely,

                                  _____
                                  (Signature)

                                  _____
                                  (Type or print name)

                                  _____
                                  (Relationship to deceased)

                                  _____
                                  (Type or print address)

(Send "Certified Mail - Return Receipt Requested")

Sample Letter
For
Social Security Benefits

How To Claim
Social Security Benefits
Due You

SAMPLE LETTER TO SOCIAL SECURITY ADMINISTRATOR OBTAIN ADDRESS FROM FUNERAL DIRECTOR OF TELEPHONE LOCAL SS OFFICE

TO: FROM

_____   _____

_____   _____

_____   _____

_____   _____

_____   _____

I understand my Funeral Director has advised you of the death of
_____ on _____
       (Full Name)   (Date)
Social Security Number:. _____ .

As the surviving spouse, I would like to meet with one of your representatives to discuss any benefits due me.

Please schedule me for an appointment preferable on _____
                                                 (time and date)
or_____ .
      (alternate time and date)

I have available and shall bring with me certified copies of the Death Certificate, our marriage certificate, our birth certificates as well as those of our dependent children, and our Social Security cards. If anything else is needed please inform me.

                                      Sincerely,

                                      _____
                                      (Signature)

                                      _____
                                      (Type or print name)

                                      _____
                                      (Type or print address)

(Send "Certified Mail - Return Receipt Requested")

NOTE: Sometimes a telephone call to the nearest Social Security Office may be sufficient in lieu of a letter.

Sample Letter
For Benefits
From
Personal Insurance Companies
For Deceased
Federal & Non-Federal
Annuitants

REQUIREMENTS FOR OBTAINING
PERSONAL LIFE INSURANCE BENEFITS

PRIVATE LIFE INSURANCE

Normally life insurance companies require only two forms to establish proof of a claim: (1) A Statement of claim and (2) Proof of death (Certified copy of Death Certificate, or attending physician's statement).

Claim must be filed by the person legally entitled to the proceeds of the insurance, who must state in what capacity the claim is made: named beneficiary, assignee, executor, administrator, guardian, trustee, etc. Claimant must normally supply the insurance company with the following:

1. Insurance Policy Number.
2. Full name and address of deceased.
3. Decedent's occupation and date last worked.
4. Decedent's date and place of birth.
5. Date, place and cause of death.
6. Claimant's name, age, address, and Social Security number.

Contact should be made with local life insurance agent or home office to obtain necessary forms and expedite payment of claim. If no local agent is available, write insurance company. Survivors should be careful not to discard any document, such as insurance policies, even when it is thought to have elapsed. Inquire of the insurer whether any benefits are due under the policy.

If decedent was a participant in the (FBI) Society insurance program, contact should be made with Society headquarters.

If decedent was a member of any union, service organization, business association, fraternal organization, or automobile club, the group should be contacted for information as to any insurance or other benefits available to survivors.

If decedent was employed at time of death, contact his place of employment regarding group life insurance, pension fund contributions, credit union balance or insurance, and other benefits. Check particularly the decedent's medical coverage with the company to determine whether spouse and dependent children are still covered.

Many insurance policies provide several payment options for receiving proceeds due the beneficiary: lump sum, life annuity or periodic payments. Insurance proceeds are not taxable nor considered income to the beneficiary.

ESTATE AND INHERITANCE TAXES

Providing specific and acceptable service that might be needed in this area is difficult at best. Laws covering such taxes will vary from state to state and both state and Federal regulations may change with irregular frequency. While many individuals might have general knowledge about taxes, they may lack the expertise necessary to assist survivors in handling tax matters of a complicated nature. However, in some instances, it might be possible to obtain competent help from a friend; otherwise, ask for suggestions as to names of trustworthy individuals known to have expertise in this field.

SAMPLE LETTER TO PERSONAL INSURANCE COMPANY

TO: FROM

Special Agents Mutual Benefit Association, Inc.
11301 Old Georgetown Road   _____
North Bethesda, MD 20852   _____
                                                              DATE: _____

RE: Notification of Death

I regret to inform you of the death of the person identified below. Please search your records to determine if the deceased was covered under any life insurance or other plans administered by SAMBA. A Certified copy of the Death Certificate is enclosed. If life insurance is payable, kindly forward the appropriate claim form to the designated beneficiary.

INFORMATION ABOUT THE DECEASED

Name: _____
SSN: _____ Date of Birth: _____
Date of Death: _____ Cause of Death: _____
_____

PERSON TO CONTACT FOR ADDITIONAL INFORMATION

Name: _____ _____
Address: _____
_____
Daytime Telephone: _____
Relationship to Deceased: _____
_____

                                                              Sincerely,

                                                              _____
                                                              (Signature)

Enclosure: Death Certificate

SAMPLE LETTER TO PERSONAL INSURANCE COMPANY

TO: FROM

_____   _____

_____   _____

_____   _____

_____   DATE: _____

RE: Death of Policy Holder

This is to advise of the death of the policy holder listed below. Please forward to the beneficiary listed below the necessary instructions required to submit a claim for proceeds of this policy and the options of settlement. Also, it would be appreciated if you would check your files for any other coverage the decedent had with your company.

Name of Deceased: _____

Residence at Time of Death:_____

Date of Death:_____ Date of Birth: _____

Social Security Number: _____

Insurance Policy Number(s): _____

Beneficiary:_____

Residence of Beneficiary:_____

_____

Sincerely,

_____
(Signature)

_____
(Relationship to Deceased)

_____
(Print Name)

_____
(Print Address)

(Send "Certified Mail - Return Receipt Requested")

Death Notification
To
Educational Institutions

DEATH NOTIFICATION FOR THE FOLLOWING
EDUCATIONAL INSTITUTION(S)
I ATTENDED

Name of Institution   Address

_____

_____

_____

_____

_____

_____

_____

_____

_____

_____

_____

_____

_____

_____

_____

_____

_____

_____

_____

_____

_____

_____

_____

_____

DEATH NOTIFICATION OF:
NAME_____

From: _____

_____

_____

_____

To: _____

_____

_____

_____

Dear Sir/Madame:

Please be advised that _____ ,
who attended _____ ,
died on _____/_____/_____.

If there is any additional information you need for record purposes, please do let me know.

Sincerely,

_____

Death Notification To Specific Organizations

DEATH NOTIFICATION FOR "SPECIFIC" ORGANIZATIONS OF WHICH I WAS A MEMBER

Name of Contact Organization	Address	"Urgent": By Phone If Checked Off X	
		( )	
		( )	
		( )	
		( )	
		( )	
		( )	
		( )	
		( )	

DEATH NOTIFICATION FOR "SPECIFIC" ORGANIZATIONS OF WHICH I WAS A MEMBER (CONT'D)

Name of Contact Organization	Address	"Urgent": By Phone If Checked Off X	
		( )	
		( )	
		( )	
		( )	
		( )	
		( )	
		( )	
		( )	

Sample Letter
To Increase
Federal Annuity Benefits

SAMPLE LETTER CAN BE USED BY BOTH FEDERAL & NON- FEDERAL EMPLOYEE

* Non-Federal - Should direct letter to human resource dept. of last employer
* When spouse predeceases annuitant

Company Name _____
Address _____

U. S. Office of Personal Management
Employee Service and Record Center
Boyers, PA 16017

RE: Retired Employee's Change in Marital Status

I elected a reduced annuity to provide survivor benefits for my spouse following my death. I am now not married and I am applying to have my annuity raised to the full amount.

Name (Please print): _____
CSA Number: _____ Date of Birth: _____
Address: _____
_____
Date of Retirement _____ Date Marriage Terminated: _____

Marriage Terminated by (Check appropriate box)
    Divorce or annulment   ( ) (Copy of final decree attached)
    Death   ( ) (Certified copy of Spouse's Death Certificate attached)

Sincerely,

_____
(Signature)

(Send "Certified Mail - Return Receipt Requested")

SAMPLE LETTER CAN BE USED BY BOTH FEDERAL & NON- FEDERAL EMPLOYEE

* Remarriage & Survivorship Benefits
* Non-Federal - Direct leter to human resource dept. of last employer

Company Name _____
Address _____

TO: DATE:

U. S. Office of Personal Management
Employee Service and Record Center
Boyers, PA 16017

RE: Retired Employee's Change in Marital Status

I originally elected a reduced annuity to provide survivor benefits for my spouse following my death. My spouse died on _____following which I was restored to full annuity. I am now remarried (or I plan to remarry) and wish to provide survivorship benefits to my new spouse. Certified copy of Marriage Certificate enclosed (or will be forwarded).

Name (Please print): _____
CSA Number: _____ Date of Birth: _____
Address:_____
_____
Date of Second Marriage: _____
Name of New Spouse: _____

To provide for this survivorship benefit, it is my understanding that I have the option of refunding to OPM an amount (plus interest) representing the difference between the amount I received while on full annuity and the amount I would have received had deductions for survivorship benefits been made, or accepting a 25% reduction in my present annuity. Please advise if I am correct in this assumption, the amount that would have to be refunded, and on what terms the payment can be made should I choose the first option.

Sincerely,

_____
(Signature)

(Send "Certified Mail - Return Receipt Requested")

GENERAL INFORMATION
SOCIAL SECURITY BENEFITS

How Do You Qualify For Retirement Benefits?

When you work and pay Social Security taxes (called FICA on some pay stubs), you earn Social Security credits. Most people earn the maximum of four credits per year.

The number of credits you need to get retirement benefits depends on your date of birth. If you were born in 1929 or later, you need 40 credits (10 years of work). People born before 1929 need fewer than 40 credits (39 credits if born in 1928; 38 credits if born in 1927; etc.

If you stop working before you have enough credits to qualify for benefits, your credits will remain on your Social Security record. If you return to work later on, you can add more credits so that you qualify. No retirement benefits can be paid until you have the required number of credits.

If you're like most people, you will earn many more credits than you need to qualify for Social Security. These extra credits do not increase your Social Security benefit. However, the income you earn while working will increase your benefit, as you will learn in the next section.

How Much Will Your Retirement Benefit Be?

Your benefit amount is based on your earnings averaged over most of your working career. Higher lifetime earnings result in higher benefits. If you have some years of no earnings or low earnings, your benefit amount may be lower than if you had worked steadily.

Your benefit amount also is affected by your age at the time you start receiving benefits. If you start your retirement benefits at age 62 (the earliest possible retirement age), your benefit will be lower than if you waited until a later age.

> *Here's An Important Point:* Social Security will give you a personalized benefit estimate at your request. Call toll-free telephone number, **1-800-772-1213**, to ask for a Form-7004, *(Request for Earnings and Benefit Estimate Statement).* Within four to six weeks after you complete and return the form to Social Security, you will receive a statement of your earnings record and estimates of your Social Security benefits for early retirement, full retirement and retirement at age 70. We'll also give you an estimate of the disability benefits you could receive if you become severely disabled before you're eligible for full retirement, as well as the amount of benefits payable to your spouse and other eligible family members due to your retirement, disability or death. If you're age 60 or older, you can get an estimate of your retirement benefits by calling our toll-free number. And, if you have access to the Internet, you can request a
> *Personal Earnings and Benefit Estimate* from SSA's web site at www.ssa.gov. Your statement will be mailed to your within four weeks.

Full Retirement Age

The usual retirement age for people retiring now is age 65. Social Security calls this "full retirement age," and the benefit amount that is payable is considered the full retirement benefit.
Because of longer life expectancies, the full retirement age will be increased in gradual steps until it reaches age 67. This change starts in the year 2003, and it affects people born in 1938 and later.

Early Retirement

You can start your Social Security benefits as early as age 62, but the benefit amount you receive will be less than your full retirement benefit.

If your take early retirement, your benefits will be permanently reduced based on the number of months you will receive checks before you reach full retirement age. If your full retirement age is 65, the reduction for starting your Social Security at age 62 is about 20 percent; at age 63 it is about 13 $1/3$ percent; and at age 64, it is about 6 $2/3$ percent.

Age To Receive Full Social Security Benefits

Year of Birth	Full Retirement Age
1937 or earlier	65
1938	65 and 2 months
1939	65 and 4 months
1940	65 and 6 months
1941	65 and 8 months
1942	65 and 0 months
1943 - 1954	66
1955	66 and 2 months
1956	66 and 4 months
1957	66 and 6 months
1958	66 and 8 months
1959	65 and 10 months
1960 and later	67

If your full retirement age is older than 65 (that is, you were born after 1937), you still will be able to take your retirement benefits at age 62, but the reduction in your benefit amount will be greater than it is for people retiring now.

Here's how it works. If your full retirement age is 67, the reduction for starting your benefits at 62 is about 30 percent; at age 63, it's about 25 percent; at age 64, about 20 percent; at age 65, about 13 $1/3$ percent; and at age 66, about 6 $2/3$ percent.

As a general rule, early retirement will give you about the same total Social Security benefits over your lifetime, but in smaller amounts to take into account the longer period you will receive them.

Some people stop working before they reach age 62. In that case, it's important to remember that during years with no earnings, you miss the opportunity to increase your benefit amount by replacing lower earnings years with higher earnings years.

Here's An Import Point: sometimes poor health forces people to retire early. If you are unable to continue working because of poor health, you should consider applying for Social Security disability benefits. The amount of the disability benefit is the same as a full, unreduced retirement benefit. If you are receiving Social Security disability benefits when you reach age 65, they will be converted to retirement benefits. For more information, call us to ask for a copy of the booklet, *Disability Benefits* (Publication No. 05-10029).

Delayed Retirement

Not everyone retires at full retirement age. You may decide to continue working full time beyond that time. In that case, you can increase your Social Security benefit in two ways.

● Each additional year you work adds another year of earnings to your Social Security record. Higher lifetime earnings may result in higher benefits when your retire.

● In addition, your benefit will be increased by a certain percentage if you delay retirement. These increases will be added in automatically from the time you reach your full retirement age until you start taking your benefits, or you reach age 70. The percentage varies depending on your year of birth. See the chart below for the increase that will apply to you.

For example, if you were born in 1943 or later, we will add eight percent per year (2/3 of 1 percent per month) to your benefit for each year you delay signing up for Social Security beyond your full retirement age.

Increases For Delayed Retirement

Year of Birth	Yearly Rate Of Increase
1917 - 1924	3%
1925 - 1926	3.5%
1927 - 1928	4%
1929 - 1930	4.5%
1931 - 1932	5%
1933 - 1934	5.5%
1935 - 1936	6%
1937 - 1938	6.5%
1939 - 1940	7%
1941 - 1942	7.5%

1943 or later	8%

Here's An Important Point: If you decide to delay your retirement, **be sure to sign up for Medicare at age 65**. In some circumstances, medical insurance costs more if you delay applying for it

Choosing Your Retirement Date

If you plan to start your retirement benefits after age 62, it is a good idea to contact Social Security in advance to see which month is best to claim benefits. In some cases, your choice of a retirement month could mean additional benefits for you and your family.

It may be to your advantage to have your Social Security benefits start in January, even if you don't plan to retire until later in the year. Depending on your earnings and your benefit amount, it may be possible for you to start collecting benefits even though you continue to work. Under current rules, many people can receive the most benefits possible with an application that is effective in January.

If you are not working, or your annual earnings are under the earnings limits, or your plan to start collecting your Social Security when you turn 62, you should apply for benefits three months before the date you want your benefits to start.

Because the rules are complicated, we urge you to discuss your plans with Social Security claims representative in the year *before* the year you plan to retire.

Retirement Benefits for Widow(er)s

Widow(er)s can begin receiving benefits at age 60 or age 50 if disabled. If you are receiving widows or widowers (including divorced widows or widowers) benefits, you can switch to your own retirement benefits - assuming you're eligible and your retirement rate is higher than your widower's rate - as early as age 62. In many cases, a widow(er) can begin receiving one benefit at a reduced rate and then switch to the other benefits at an unreduced rate at age 65. The rules vary depending on the situation, so you should talk to a Social Security representative about the options available to you.

ABOUT FAMILY BENEFITS

Benefits For Family Members

If you're receiving retirement benefits, some members of your family also can receive benefits. Those who can included:

- your wife or husband age 62 or older;

- your wife or husband under age 62, if she or he is taking care of your child who is under age 16 or disabled;

- your former wife or husband age 62 or older

- children up to age 18

- children age 18-19, if they are full-time students through grade 12; and

- children over age 18, if they are disabled.

Spouse's Benefits

A spouse receives one-half of the retired worker's full benefit unless the spouse begins collecting benefits before age 65. In that case, the amount of the spouse's benefit is permanently reduced by a percentage based on the number of months before she or he reaches 65. For example, if your spouse begins collecting benefits at 64, the benefit amount would be about 46 percent of your full benefit. At age 63, it would be about 42 percent, and 37.5 percent at age 62. However, if your spouse is taking care of a child who is under age 16 or disabled and receiving Social Security benefits, your spouse gets full benefits, regardless of age.

If you're eligible for both your own retirement benefits and for benefits as a spouse, we always pay your own benefit first. If your benefit as a spouse is higher than your retirement benefit, you'll get a combination of benefits equaling the higher spouse benefit.

Here's an example:

Mary Ann qualifies for a retirement benefit of $250 and a wife's benefit of $400. At age 65, when will receive her own $250 retirement benefit and we will add $150 from her wife's benefit, for a total of $400. If she takes her retirement benefit at any time before she turns 65, both amounts will be reduced.

Maximum Family Benefits

If you have children eligible for Social Security, each will receive up to one-half of your full benefit. But there is a limit to the amount of money that can be paid to a family. If the total benefits due your spouse and children exceed this limit, their benefits will be reduced proportionally. Your benefit will not be affected.

Benefits For A Divorced Spouse

A divorced spouse can get benefits on a former husband's or wife's Social Security record if the marriage lasted at least 10 years. The divorced spouse must be 62 or older and unmarried. If the spouse has been divorced at least two years, he or she can get benefits, even if the worker is not retired. However, the worker must have enough credits to qualify for benefits and be age 62 or older. The amount of benefits a divorced spouse gets has no effect on the amount of benefits a current spouse can get.

WHAT YOU NEED TO KNOW WHEN YOU'RE ELIGIBLE FOR RETIREMENT BENEFITS

How do You Sign Up For Social Security?

You can call toll-free number, **1-800-772-1213**, to apply for benefits or to make an appointment to visit any Social Security office to apply in person.

Depending on your circumstances, you will need some or all of the documents listed below. But don't delay applying for benefits because you don't have all the information. If you don't have a document you n need, we can help you get it.

Information Needed:
- your Social Security number;

- your birth certificate;

- your W-2 forms or self-employment tax return for last year;

- your military discharge papers if you had military service;

- your spouses's birth certificate and Social Security number if he or she is applying for benefits;

- children's birth certificates and Social Security numbers, if applying for children's benefits;

- proof of U.S. citizenship or lawful alien status if you (or a spouse or child is applying for benefits) were not born in the U.S. and

- the name of your bank and your account number so your benefits can be directly deposited into your account.

You will need to submit original documents or copies certified by the issuing office. You can mail or bring them to Social Security. We will make photocopies and return your documents.

Right To Appeal

If you disagree with a decision made on your claim, you can appeal it. The steps you can take are explained in the factsheet, *The Appeals Process* (Publication No. 05-10041), which is available from Social Security.

You have the right to represented by an attorney or other qualified person of your choice. More information is in the factsheet, *Your Right To Representation* (Publication No. 05-10075), which also is available form Social Security.

If You Work And Get Social Security At The Same Time

You can continue to work and still get retirement benefits. Earnings in, or after, the month you reach age 70 won't affect your Social Security benefits. However, before age 70, your benefits will be reduced if your earnings exceed certain limits.

- **If you are under 65**, $1 in benefits will be deducted for each $2 in earnings above the limit.

- **If you are 65 through 69**, $1 in benefits will be deducted for each $3 in earnings above the limit.

These limits increase each year as average wages increase. For the current amounts, contact Social Security to ask for the leaflet, *How Work Affects Your Benefits* (Publication No. 05-10069).

If other family members receive benefits on your Social Security record, the total family benefits will be affected by your earnings. This means we will offset not only your benefits, but those payable to your family as well. If a family member works, however, the family member's earnings affect only his or her benefits.

If during the year, your earnings are higher or lower than you estimated, let us know as soon as possible so we can adjust your benefits.

A Special Monthly Rule

A special rule applies to your earnings for one year, usually your first year of retirement. Under this rule, you can receive a full Social Security check for any **month** you are "retired," regardless of your yearly earnings. Your earnings must be under a monthly limit. If you're self-employed, the services you perform in your business are taken into consideration as well.

If you want more information on how earnings affect your retirement benefit, call us to ask for a copy of the leaflet, *How Work Affects Your Benefits* (Publication No. 05-10069). This leaflet has the figures for the current annual and monthly earnings limits.

Your Benefits May Be Taxable

About 20 percent of people who get Social Security have to pay taxes on their benefits. This provision affects only people who have substantial income in addition to their Social Security.

At the end of each year, you will receive a *Social Security Benefit Statement* (Form SSA-1099) in the mail showing the amount of benefits you received. You can use this statement when you are completing your federal income tax return to find out if any of your benefits are subject to tax.

For more information, call the Internal Revenue Service's toll-free telephone number, 1-800-829-3676, to ask for Publication 554, *Tax Information for Older Americans*, and Publication 915, *Social Security Benefits and Equivalent Railroad Retirement Benefits*.

Pensions From Work Not Covered by Social Security

If you get a pension from work where you paid Social Security taxes, it will **not** affect your Social Security benefits. However, if you get a pension from work that was not covered by Social Security - for example, the federal civil service, some state or local government employment or work in a foreign country - your Social Security benefit may be lowered or offset - for more information, call Social Security to ask for the factsheets, *Government Pension Offset* - for government workers who may be eligible for Social security benefits on the record of a husband or wife (Publication No. 05-10007) - and a *Pension From Work Not Covered by Social Security* - for people who worked in another country or for government workers who also are eligible for their own Social Security benefits (Publication No. 05-10045).

Leaving the United States

If you are a united States citizen, you can travel or live in most foreign countries without affecting your eligibility for Social Security benefits. However, there are a few countries - Cambodia, Cuba, North Korea, Vietnam and many of the former U.S.S.R. republics (except Estonia, Latvia, Lithuania, and Russia) - where we cannot send Social Security checks.

If you work outside the United States, different rules apply in determining if you can get your benefit checks.

Most people who are neither U.S. residents nor U.S. citizens will have 25.5. percent of their benefits withheld for federal income tax.

For more information, call us to ask for a copy of the booklet, *Your Social Security Payments While You Are Outside The United States* (Publication No. 05-10137).

SOCIAL SECURITY'S FUTURE...AND YOURS!

Many people wonder where their Social Security tax dollars go. Generally, out of every dollar you pay in Social Security taxes:

- 70 cents goes to a trust fund that pays monthly benefits to retirees and their families and to widows, widowers and children of workers who have died;

- 19 cents goes to a trust fund that pays for the health care of all Medicare beneficia ries; and

- 11 cents goes to a trust fund that pays benefits to people with disabilities and their families.

Your Social Security taxes also pay for administering Social Security. The administrative costs are paid from the trust funds described above and are **less than one cent** of every Social Security tax dollar collected.

Money not used to pay benefits and administrative expenses is invested in U.S. government bonds, generally considered the safest of all investments. The government uses the money it has borrowed from Social Security - just as it uses money you may have invested in savings bonds - to pay for all the services and projects it provides for our citizens. And just as the government pays you interest on your bonds, so will it make good on its obligations to Social Security.

You also need to know about Social Security's financial stability. Each year, Social Security's Board of Trustees reports on the financial status of the social security program. These reports are valuable tools for evaluating and ensuring the economic health of the Social Security system. The latest report indicates that the Social Security system, as currently structured, will be able to pay benefits well into the next century. This means Congress has the time it needs to make changes to safeguard the programs; financial future.

You can count on Social Security being there when you need it.

OTHER BOOKLETS AVAILABLE

- Social Security has a number of publications that contain information about other Social security programs. Contact Social Security to get a free copy of any of these publications. They include:

- Social Security - Understanding The Benefits (Publication No. 05-10024) - comprehensive explanation of all the Social Security programs;

- Social Security - Disability Benefits (Publication No. 05-10029) - explains Social Security disability benefits;

- Medicare (Publication No. 05-10043) - explains Medicare hospital insurance and medical insurance;

- Social Security - Survivors Benefits (Publication No. 05-10084) - explains Social Security survivors benefits; and

- Social Security - Supplemental Security Income (Publication No. 05-11000) - explains this program which provides a basic income to people 65 or older, disabled or blind who have limited income and resources.

Social Security's Toll-Free Number

1-800-772-1213

Internet: http://www.ssa.gov

MEDICARE/MEDICAID

A Word About Medicare

Medicare is a health insurance plan for people who are 65 or older. People who are disabled or have permanent kidney failure can get Medicare at any age.

Medicare has two parts - hospital insurance and medical insurance. Most people have both parts.

Hospital insurance, sometimes called Part A, covers inpatient hospital care and certain follow-up care. You already have paid for it as part of your Social Security taxes while you were working.

Medical insurance, sometimes called Part B, pays for physicians' services and some other services not covered by hospital insurance. Medical insurance is optional, and a premium is charge.

If you're already getting Social Security benefits when you turn 65, your Medicare (Part A) starts automatically. If you're not getting Social Security, you should sign up for Medicare close to your 65 birthday, even if you aren't ready to retire. For more information, call and ask for the booklet, *Medicare* (Publication No 05-10043).

Help For Low-Income Medicare Beneficiaries

If you have a low income and few resources, your state may pay your Medicare premiums and, in some cases, other "out-of-pocket" Medicare expenses, such as deductible and coinsurance.

Only your state can decide if you qualify for help under this program. If you think you may qualify, contact your state or local medical assistance (Medicaid) agency, social services or welfare office. For more information, contact Social Security to request a copy of the leaflet, *Medicare Savings for Qualified Beneficiaries* (HCFA Publication No. 02184)

FOR MORE INFORMATION

Recorded information and services arc available 24 hours a day, including weekends and holidays, by calling Social Security's toll-free number, **1-800-772-1213.** Your can call for an appointment or to speak to a service representative between the hours of 7 a.m. and 7 p.m. on business days. Lines are busiest early in the week and early in the month, so, if your business can wait, it's best to call at other times. Whenever you call, have your Social Security number handy.

You can also access Social Security information on the Internet at http://www.ssa.gov.

People who are deaf or hard of hearing may call our too-free "TTY" number, 1-800-325-0778, between 7 a.m. and 7 p.m. on business days.

The Social Security Administration treats all calls confidentially - whether they're made to toll-free numbers or to local offices.

THIS SECTION APPLIES TO RETIRED FEDERAL CIVIL SERVICE EMPLOYEES

SURVIVORS' BENEFITS — OFFICE OF PERSONNEL MANAGEMENT (FORMERLY CALLED U.S, CIVIL SERVICE COMMISSION)

Eligible survivors of a deceased annuitant can collect benefits under the Civil Service Retirement Act with little or no difficulty, providing they follow a four-step procedure:

(1) Notify the Office of Personnel Management, Retirement Operations Center Boyers. PA 16017. This should be done immediately after the death of an annuitant so that the Office of Personnel Management (OPM) can begin the necessary work involved without delay. The letter of notification should include the full name of the deceased annuitant, exact date of birth, exact date of death, CSA number (Civil Service Annuity number issued to annuitant at time of retirement), name, address and relationship of person apparently entitled to survivor's benefits. As soon as the OPM receives the letter, it will examine the deceased annuitant's records and send application to the individual apparently entitled to benefits.

The OPM will also provide the eligible survivor with an application for benefits under the Federal Employee Group Life Insurance Act (FEGLI) providing the deceased annuitant was covered under the program. Details concerning FEGLI are provided elsewhere in this book.

(2) Return any uncashed annuity checks payable to the decedent to: Office of Personnel Management (OPM) Employee Service and Records Center. Boyers. PA 16017. DO NOT CASH OR DEPOSIT THE CHECK. In your communication explain that the check is being returned because of the death of the annuitant, and furnish the exact date of death. This is necessary because government checks made payable to a deceased annuitant cannot legally be cashed by anyone. It is suggested that you write across the check in ink "Payee Deceased" and the date and sign the notation. The OPM will not authorize a survivor benefit until the Treasury Department informs them that there are no outstanding checks payable to the deceased annuitant. However, any accrued annuity unpaid to the annuitant during his lifetime will be included in the benefits to his eligible survivors.

If annuity payments have been sent directly to the bank or other financial institution, promptly notify the OPM and the bank of the annuitant's exact date of death. The Treasury Department will recover the amount of the deposit from the bank, who in turn will recover from the depositor.

DO NOT attempt to make individual repayment by personal check or money order to the OPM or the U.S. Treasury Department.

(3) Complete the application for survivor's annuity benefits as well as the one for benefits under the FEGLI and return in the envelopes provided with applications. Upon receipt of these applications, they will be processed and payment of benefits due will be authorized. It is pointed out that these benefits may include automatic health insurance coverage if the survivor has been covered by the annuitant's enrollment in one of the government's Health Benefit Programs and if the survivor is eligible for a survivor annuity beginning immediately after the death of the annuitant.

(4) Include a certified copy of the annuitant's death certificate with applications for benefits. The OPM requires proof of the exact date of annuitant's death, therefore a certified copy of the death certificate should accompany the application for survivor's annuity and a certified copy of the death certificate should be attached to the application for benefits under the Federal Employees Group Life Insurance Act. If other evidence is required to support claims for benefits, the OPM will request it. This could include: copy of marriage certificate, birth certificates, divorce decrees, or other documents establishing identity or relationship.

RESTORATION OF TOTAL ANNUITY

If at the time of retirement a retiree elected survivor's benefits, a percentage of his or her annuity is withheld each month to offset the cost of an annuity to be paid to a surviving spouse when the retiree dies. Since October 26, 1974, with the enactment of public law 93-474, those retirees who have lost their survivor spouse are eligible to have that reduction for survivor's benefits restored to their annuity. The OPM should be notified of a change in martial status to effect restoration. Include the following information:

(1)   Name of retiree.
(2)   CSA Number.
(3)   Date of birth of retiree.
(4)   Address.
(5)   Date of retirement.
(6)   Date of marriage terminated.
(7)   Reasons for termination: death, divorce. Include copy of spouse's
          death certificate or copy of final divorce decree.

In the event of remarriage the retiree should notify OPM so that reduction can be reinstituted to restore survivor's benefits for the new spouse.

THERE ARE TWO NEW FEATURES TO THE FEDERAL EMPLOYEES' GROUP LIFE INSURANCE (FEGLI) PROGRAM:

LIVING BENEFITS

Effective July 25, 1995, annuitants who have a life expectancy of 9 months or less and are enrolled in the FEGLI Program may elect Living Benefits. If you receive Living Benefits, you Basic insurance amount (with certain reductions) will be paid to you in a lump-sum before your death. No Basic insurance benefits would be payable to your survivor(s) or beneficiary(ies) after your death. Your physician must complete a part of the Living Benefits claim form regarding your life expectancy

If you are enrolled in the FEGLI Program, your coverage automatically includes this new Living Benefits feature. You do not need to take any action at this time unless you are terminally ill and wish to elect this benefit. If you elect Living Benefits, you may not assign your life insurance coverage. An election of Living Benefits does not affect any optional you may have. You may only elect Living Benefits once during your lifetime.

If you are terminally ill and believe you qualify for and wish to elect Living Benefits, please write to: Office of Federal Employees' Group Life Insurance
Park Avenue, New York, NY 10166-0188

Please be sure to include your full name, CSA number, phone number and address.

ASSIGNMENT

You may assign your life insurance coverage to another person or persons, including an individual, a corporation or an irrevocable trust. Assignment means that you transfer ownership and control of your Basic, Option A and Option B insurance (if you have these coverages) to the assignee(s). Thereafter, life insurance premiums will continue to be withheld from your annuity. You will not be able to cancel your insurance or cancel the assignment. If you assign your life insurance coverage, you may not then or thereafter designate beneficiaries for your insurance and all prior designations become void. The assignee(s) become(s) the beneficiary (unless he/she designates someone else). Option C (family optional) insurance may not be assigned.

Assignments are generally made to comply with a court order upon divorce, for inheritance tax purposes, to obtain cash before death from a viatical settlement firm (for terminally ill individuals), or to satisfy a debt. The decision to assign life insurance's coverage is yours alone. If you assign your insurance, you may not elect Living Benefits

If you would like to request an assignment form (RI 76-10), which contains more information, please write to: Office of Personnel Management
Retirement Operations Center
Attention: RI 76-10, Boyers, PA 16017

Please be sure to include your full name, CSA number, phone number and address.

FEDERAL EMPLOYEES GROUP LIFE INSURANCE PROGRAM

An annuitant may have life insurance coverage under the Federal Employees Group Life Insurance Act (FEGLI) only if he meets all the following requirements:

1. Retired after August, 1954, the effective date of the Life Insurance Act, and was awarded an annuity which commenced within 31 days after separation from Federal Civilian Service.

2. Was covered under the Life Insurance Act as an employee and did not convert to an individual like insurance policy upon retirement.

3. Retired under the total disability provision or had at least 15 years of creditable service if his retirement was before September 23, 1959, or at least 12 years of creditable service if his retirement was after September 23, 1959.

FEGLI offers regular and optional insurance. Regular insurance coverage depends on annual basic pay. The minimum amount is $10,000 and the maximum is $60,000. If an employee had regular insurance, he could elect optional insurance in the amount of $10,000. The U.S. Government pays one-third of the cost of regular insurance and the Federal employee pays the other two-thirds. The full cost of optional insurance is paid by the employee and depends on age. The premium increases at ages 35, 40, 45, 55, and 60.

Both the regular and optional insurance can be continued after retirement on an immediate annuity. You do not pay premiums for regular insurance after retirement but it is necessary to pay optional insurance premiums until you reach age 65, if you retire before that age. When you retire at age 65 or over, or when you reach age 65 if you retire before that age, both the regular and optional life insurance coverage reduces by 2% a month until a reduction of 75% is reached. At the time a Federal employee retires he is issued a statement by the OPM explaining his monthly annuity and showing the amount of insurance coverage he has under FEGLI.

When an annuitants dies, FEGLI is paid in the order of precedence as follows:

1. To the beneficiary designated by the insured.

2. If there is no such beneficiary, to the widow or widower.

3. If none of the above, to the child or children of insured with the share of any deceased child distributed among decedents of that child.

4. If none of the above, 10 the parents of the insured or the survivor of them.

5. If none of the above, to the executor or administrator of the insured's estate.

6. If none of the above, to the other next of kin of the insured entitled under the laws of domicile of the insured at the time of death.

Changes in beneficiaries under FEGLI can be made at any time and probably should be if retired is not survived by a spouse.

THIS SECTION APPLIES TO
RETIRED STATE CIVIL SERVICE EMPLOYEES

The retirement system is most states usually covers all *Public Employees*, including *Police* and *Firemen.*

In most cases, the division of pensions and benefits is assigned all administrative functions of the retirement system except for investment.

All members who are in good standing in their respective retirement system should have in their possession a handbook which contains all the pertinent information concerning retirement, types of retirement, enrollments, health benefits programs, general information and death benefits etc...each of these topics and their subheadings are numerically identified, so that should you be interested in obtaining additional information about any of the topics, a phone call can be made to a specifies phone number mentioned in the handbook. For example: if you reside in the state of New Jersey, the retirement handbook indicates that one should call the division of pensions and benefits' information library at (609) 777-1931. The caller will be given instructions on the use of the library. By using the three digit number preceding you particular topic of interest, you will be given access to the prerecorded information on that topic.

A survivor or beneficiary of a deceased state civil servant can obtain all the necessary information pertaining to death benefits by accessing the prerecorded data as outlined in the retirement handbook.

Further, the survivor or beneficiary may wish to receive by mail, information about several retirement topics including death benefits, and may do so by complying with the instructions set out in the retirement handbook.

FEDERAL RETIREMENT SERVICES BY TELEPHONE

YOUR GUIDE TO NEW TOLL-FREE AND AUTOMATED SERVICES

NOW ENJOY EASIER ACCESS TO YOUR RETIREMENT ACCOUNT

Using an automated system, the **Retirement Information Office** (RIO) now allows you to:

- Make Federal Tax Elections
- Make State Tax Elections
- Request Verification of Your Income
- Request the Value to Your Life Insurance
- Request Verification of the Civil Service Retirement survivor benefits you are providing
- Request OPM retirement Forms and Brochures

How Do I access the Retirement Information Office?

Using a touch-tone telephone, call **88 US OPM RET** (888 767-6738) and follow the menu choices. Please note that this is a new toll-free telephone number that replaces the (202) 606-0500 number.

When can I access the Retirement Information Office?

The Retirement Information Office automated system is available seven days a week, 22 hours a day. The system is down from 2 AM to 4 AM Eastern Time (ET) and occasionally on weekends for system updates.

Will I be able to speak to a Customer Service Specialist?

Yes. Customer Service Specialists are available from 7:30 AM to 5:30 PM ET. If you have a rotary telephone, just stay on the line and the next available Customer Service Specialist will assist you. If you have a touch-tone telephone, you will be given the option of speaking with a Customer Service Specialist throughout the menu.

I don't have a touch-tone telephone, can I use a rotary telephone?

You must have a touch-tone telephone to use the automated features of the Retirement Information Office telephone system. If you have a rotary telephone, a Customer Service Specialist will be available to assist you.

I'm hearing Impaired, can I use the Retirement Information Office Automated System?

Yes, the automated system is capable of assisting TDD callers. Call us toll-free at (800) 878-5707.

How do I obtain my PIN, and how do I change my PIN?

Just call the Retirement Information Office and follow the instructions for obtaining or changing your PIN.

What if I lose or forget my PIN?

Call the Retirement Information Office and ask to speak with a Customer Service Specialist. The Specialist will ask you identifying information and then allow you to establish a new PIN.

What if someone else uses my PIN to make changes to my account?

You are responsible for safeguarding your PIN. If you feel that someone else has used your PIN to make a change to your account, call the Retirement Information Office immediately. Change your PIN and then ask to speak with a Customer Service Specialist. We will work with you to correct any unauthorized changes to your account.

How will I know when a requested action is effective?

When you make a change to your account using the automated system, the system will verify the information you have entered before you complete the transaction. The system will also tell you when the requested change will take effect. Your requested change will be held by the system until records are updated that evening.

What information do I need before I call the Retirement Information Office?

You must have your CSA or CSF annuity claim number and your PIN number.

What if I don't like dealing with "talking computers"?

We have designed the Retirement Information Office system to be easy to use. You will be guided through each process and will always be able to return to the previous menu.

The system will enable you to perform many transactions without the need to speak with a Customer Service Specialist.

Will the Retirement Information Office continue to expand?

Yes, if we receive comments or suggestions from you. We will base future expansion and improvements on your suggestions. We will also monitor the usage to determine if more telephone lines are needed. We hope you find the system to be a valuable service.

Where should I send my comments?

We will periodically conduct customer surveys to determine your satisfaction with the RIO automated system. If you would like to send comments about the system, write:

US Office of Personnel Management
Retirement Services Division
1900 E Street, NW
Room 1312
Washington, DC 20414-0001

Email: retire@opm.gov

UNITED STATES OFFICE OF PERSONNEL MANAGEMENT
POST OFFICE BOX 45
BOYERS, PA 16017-0045

The Office of Personnel Management has an automated system to assist you when calling the Retirement Information Office (RIO). The RIO is your point of contact for assistance by telephone with retirement inquiries. We have enclosed information on previous pages that gives you a detailed list of new functions and answers questions about using the system. We have also enclosed information on the U.S. Treasury's Savings Bond Program.

Your New Personal Identification Number (PIN)

To make the system as secure as possible, we have created a randomly selected PIN for each annuitant and survivor annuitant. Your PIN is located in the upper right hand corner of this letter in the shaded area. Please keep this PIN in a safe place and do not allow anyone else access to your PIN. Once you use the system, you will be able to change the PIN if you wish. Many new changes can be made to your retirement account, and only your should have the ability to make these changes.

The RIO automated system is designed for callers with touch-tone telephones. If you do not have a touch-tone telephone, a Customer service Specialist will be available to assist you. The system has also been designed to allow the hearing impaired to communicate through a Telecommunications Device for the Deaf (TDD).

When you dial the RIO, the automated telephone system will present you with an introductory menu to determine the nature of your call. The first two selections on the introductory menu, reporting the death of an annuitant or survivor, or reporting a missing payment, do not require a PIN. The third selection on the introductory menu should be selected if you are calling OPM about any other matter. Once you make this selection, you will be prompted for your claim number and PIN (if you need to obtain a new PIN, you will be given the option at this point). After you enter this information, you will be presented with another short menu with four selections that will allow you to make certain changes to your annuity account or request information

RIO Menus

The *first* selection allows you to make changes to your annuity account, including Federal and State tax withholdings, and address changes. Follow the prompts and you can quickly make changes to your annuity account without having to speak to a Customer Service Specialist.

The **second** selection allows you to get up-to-date information on your retirement benefits. Our new system can mail to your home address or fax to any number you supply us, information you routinely request from OPM, without having to speak to a Customer Service Specialist. The menu allows you to choose from a verification of your life insurance amount. Although we know most of you do not have a fax machine in your home, you may want to send information, such as a verification of income, to a third party, such as a Mortgage Company. Just have the fax number of the Mortgage Company available before you call, enter it when prompted, and everything is taken care of in one quick call.

The **third** selection gives you quick access to OPM information and forms. Here you will be able to request a replacement CSA or CSF annuity card, various OPM forms and pamphlets, or a duplicate 1099R statement. The system will accept your request and promptly mail our the information.

The **fourth** selection will transfer you to a Customer Service Specialist. This option is provided for matters that cannot be handled directly by the automate system. We encourage you to use the new automated system. If you encounter difficulties in using the system, a Customer Service Specialist will be available to assist you.

FEDERAL ANNUITANT EXPRESS

In January, 1996 we introduced OPM's toll-free customer service. Annuitant Express. Annuitant Express allows callers to make changes to their Federal income tax withholding without having to complete a form, write a letter or make a toll call to OPM. The service is available 24 hours a day, seven days a week.

We are happy to announce that we are expanding Annuitant Express, a service that many of you have told us is convenient and easy to use, to include State income tax withholdings and U.S. Savings Bonds. As of July 1, 1997 you will be able to start, change or stop your State income tax withholding without having to contact your state income tax office. You will also be able to make elections for the Government's Savings Bond Program.

You must use a touch-tone telephone to access Annuitant Express. Just dial 1-800-409-6528 and follow the directions given. Before you call, please be sure you have your CSA or CSF retirement claim number, your Social security Number and the two letter abbreviation an dial pad equivalent listed on the attached sheet for your state.

Since we expect most calls to be about tax withholding, we have outlined the script you will hear for state tax withholding (see next page). If you select a Savings Bond transaction your call will be handled differently.

Annuitant Express is a toll-free automated system for touch-tone telephones. If you need to talk to a Customer Service Specialist at OPM on other retirement matters, or don't have touch-tone telephone, call (202) 606-0500 Monday through Friday from 7:30 am to 5:30 pm Eastern Standard Time.

FEDERAL ANNUITANT EXPRESS
INFORMATION REQUESTED BY SYSTEM

After entering the information requested by the system to identify you, the system now needs to determine if you are calling about Federal tax withholdings or State tax withholdings.

If you would like to change your Federal income tax withholding, press 1
If you would like to change your State income tax withholding, press 2

IF YOU CURRENTLY HAVE STATE TAX WITHHELD, YOU WILL HEAR:

You currently have State tax withheld for the state of (your state), in the amount of (your withhold)

The voice prompt will give you two options:

If you would like to change or cancel the amount of your State tax withholding, press 1

If you would like to change your State tax withholding from your current state to another state, press 2

If you press 1, the voice prompt will tell you:

Please enter the whole dollar amount to be withheld from your monthly annuity payment (to cancel your State tax withholding, enter "0")

If you press 2, the voice prompt will tell you:

Please enter the two digits on your telephone which represent the two letter abbreviation of the state for which you would like to have income tax withheld* (the system will then request the whole dollar amount to be withheld, e.g. $25.00 would be 25).

IF YOU DO NOT CURRENTLY HAVE STATE TAX WITHHELD AND YOU WANT TO BEGIN WITHHOLDING, YOU WILL HEAR:

Please enter the two digits on your telephone which represent the two letter abbreviation of the state from which you would like to have income tax withheld.

Please enter the whole dollar amount of State income tax you would like withheld from your monthly annuity payment.

Once you have indicated that the amount is correct, the voice prompt will tell you when we will begin to deduct the dollar amount you requested and thank you for using Annuitant Express. This amount will remain in effect until you make a new election.

ABBREVIATION AND DIAL PAD EQUIVALENTS

Jurisdiction	Abbreviation	Dial Pad Code
Alabama	AL	25
Arizona	AZ	20
Arkansas	AR	27
California	CA	22
Colorado	CO	26
Connecticut	CT	28
Delaware	DE	33
District of Columbia	DC	32
Georgia*	GA	42
Hawaii	HI	44
Idaho	ID	43
Illinois	IL	45
Indiana	IN	46
Iowa*	IA	42
Kansas	KS	57
Kentucky	KY	59
Louisiana	LA	52
Maine*	ME	63
Maryland*	MD	63
Massachusetts*	MA	62
Michigan*	MI	64
Minnesota*	MN	66
Mississippi*	MS	67
Missouri*	MO	66
Montana	MT	68
Nebraska*	NE	63
New Jersey*	NJ	65
New Mexico*	NM	66
New York	NY	69

ABBREVIATION AND DIAL PAD EQUIVALENTS

Jurisdiction	Abbreviation	Dial Pad Code
North Carolina	NC	62
North Dakota*	ND	63
Ohio*	OH	64
Oklahoma*	OK	65
Oregon*	OR	67
Pennsylvania*	PA	72
Rhode Island	RI	74
South Carolina*	SC	72
Utah*	UT	88
Vermont*	VT	88
Virginia	VA	82
West Virginia	WV	98
Wisconsin	WI	94

Only States that have income taxes are listed above. Some states with income taxes do not tax pensions. In order to be included in Annuitant Express, states had to sign an agreement with us. If your state is not participating in Annuitant Express, the system will let you know.

* The following is an example of a "tree" that you will hear if you enter a two digit state code that corresponds to more than one state.

The code 63 represents more than one state. Please make a selection from the following list for the state you wish to have tax withheld.

For Maine, press 1
For Maryland, press 2
For Nebraska, press 3
For North Dakota, press 4

ADDITIONAL INFORMATION
REGARDING FEDERAL RETIREES

Recent laws provide that Federal retirees, whose annuities and/or other death benefits are insufficient to cover the cost of their health insurance premiums, may elect to make direct payments to OPM, rather than have premiums withheld from their annuities.

Employees under the **Federal Employees Retirement System** (FERS) were provided with a Thrift Savings Plan, which has now been extended to civil Service Retirement employees. This plan is administered by the **Federal Retirement Thrift Board, not** OPM. Therefor, a separate notification of the annuitant or survivor's death must be made to the Board at the National Finance Center, New Orleans, LA, (504) 235-6000, when such money is being paid or is due.

If a widow or former spouse of a deceased Federal retiree has been receiving survivor benefits, a non-spousal survivor should notify OPM (202) 606-0133 and, if appropriate, the **Federal Retirement Thrift Board** (504) 255 -6600. Give the deceased spouse's name, **CSF** number and date the spouse died.

When notified of the death of the spouse of a retired Federal employee, OPM does not automatically change enrollment under the **Federal Employees Health Benefits** (FEHB) plan, from self-and-family to self-only. It will be necessary to write to OPM's Health Insurance Office, Annuitant's Services division, P. O Box 14172, Washington, DC 20044, requesting Standard Form 2809, Health Benefits Registration From, in order to make the change. If you can certify that your spouse was your last eligible family member, OPM will make the change to self-only, retroactive to the day after your spouse's death and refund any premiums improperly paid.

Public Law 103-66, effective October 1, 1993, changes the method of providing a survivorship annuity to a second spouse, The choice of making a lump-sum payment, or electing to have the retiree's annuity reduced 25%, has been eliminated. Substitute for this prior option is an actuarial deduction from the retiree's annuity based on the deposit that would have been made under the old system and the age of the annuitant. It is expected in most cases to be less than 5%, plus the amount (approximately 10%) the annuity is reduced by the regular formula for electing the survivor benefit. However, the maximal reduction is 25%.

Annuitants who are now in the 25% cycle will be automatically switched to the new method, the amount of deposit still owed being spread over the expected lifetime of the annuitant; this in most cases will substantially reduce the amount of deduction. Such annuitants will be notified by OPM/.

OFFICE OF PERSONNEL MANAGEMENT
DIRECTORY FOR ASSISTANCE

CORRESPONDENCE:

Concerning matters relating to: Retirement, Insurance, and Survivor Benefits: (Use zip code, box # if any, as shown)

U. S Office of Personnel Management
Retirement Operations Center
Box 45
Boyers, PA 16017

Change of Address: P.O. Box 440 Direct deposit requests:
(Use form SF 199A available at your bank.   Zip #: 16017-0040

Reporting a Death: P.O. Box 445
Special Phone # for DEATHS ONLY:
(412-794-5216) Follow-up with letter.

Social Security Benefits for Federal   P.O. Box 200
Employees Retirement System (FERS)   Zip # 16017-0200
Disability or survivor benefits.
Does not apply to retirees under
the Civil Service System.

Report changes in Workers' Compensation   P.O. Box 45
benefit status.   Zip # 16017-0045
Obtain retirement or life insurance beneficiary
designation information.
Report Changes in Social Security benefits
paid to CSRS Off/set retiree/survivors.

FOR ALL OTHER MATTERS WRITE TO:
U.S. Office of Personnel Management
P.O. Box (see topics below for box
Washington,, D.C. 20044

Tax Election Forms (W4PA) .... P.O. Box 961
State/Federal Tax of Allotment Inquiries .... P.O. Box 989
Garnishment/Court Orders .... P.O. Box 17
General Health Benefit Inquiries .... P.O. Box 14172
Marital Status Survey, Earnings Survey Responses ...... P.O. Box 579
Deposit, Redeposit, Overpayment, Voluntary .... P.O. Box 7125
Contribution Checks
(Include claim # on Check)

Adult Student Certification .... P.O. Box 956
Disputed Insurance Claim Inquiries .... P.O. Box 436
Lost Checks/Nonreceipt (include date of ck) .... P.O. Box 78915

A WILL
AND
WHAT IT MEANS

Preparing a will is the first step towards overcoming this lack of knowledge. It is the beginning of effective financial planning. Preparing a will is neither too complicated, nor too overwhelming a task for anyone to undertake. Failure to do so, however, will often times lead to situations where effective control over financial affairs is lost. Similarly, an outdated will, or one that fails to reflect what is important can create great problems following a death.

Simply, a will is legal document providing specific written instructions or directions for the distribution of your property after your death. The objectives of your life are effectively safeguarded in this document. The preparation of your will is significantly easier if you follow a step-by-step process. Moreover, by following the process outlined below will actually discover that you have more possessions of value than you thought.

First, set aside sometime when you can be undisturbed and when you can think, or preferably write about who and what is important to you. You may also wish to share your ideas with a close friend or relative who is able to listen and serve as a sounding board before you seek professional guidance.

Ask yourself the following questions:

- What dreams do you have for yourself and for those close to you?
- What aspirations do you have for your own life?
- What are your life's goals and objectives?
- Who would you consider assigning to act as executor?
- Who might be a guardian if you have minor children?
- What relative or close friend may require special attention because of age or health?
- What people would you like to consider in planning your will?
- How would you like to include them in your will?
- What do you anticipate are their future needs?
- What are the significant issues which concern you and what organizations respond to them?
- Which organizations would you consider including as beneficiaries?
- Identify your personal assets. Consider the following:
    real estate
    stocks
    bonds
    checking accounts
    savings accounts
    holding of mortgages, notes, contracts, others

personal possessions such as:

jewelry
furs
furnishings
art works
hobby collections
autos
boats
apparel
books
other assets such as:
business interests
shares in trust funds
insurance and annuities
employee benefits.

WHAT YOU HAVE WHEN YOU HAVE FINISHED

When you have completed this inventory you have prepared a statement about your life. Your will is the legal reflection of that statement. It projects your concerns into the future.

What you have identified in this process is your estate, which exists while you are alive and after you are dead. Your next step is to analyze your debts and whatever other liabilities you may have sustained such as pledges, etc.

It is now time for you to deal with a lawyer. The assistance of an attorney assures that your will adequately reflects your best interests. Depending on the size of your estate, your lawyer might counsel you to consult with an accountant, financial advisor, a stock broker, a life insurance representative, or a trust officer. Remember, these consultants are there to aid you and they can only accomplish this if you clearly communicate your objectives to them.

It is often prudent to review your own written materials prior to meeting with these consultants for it will give you additional time to consider how you would like your possessions distributed.

The will also permits you, rather than some arbitrary set of laws, to assign an executor. An executor is the person - a friend, relative, or a professional - or the institution, your bank for instance, who manages and settles your estate according to your directions. If you fail to appoint an executor, the State might select someone to manage your affairs who neither knows, nor can act based upon your particular interests or concerns. The appointment of an administrator may also mean a formal accounting of assets which can drain extra funds from your estate.

In writing your will you may also name a guardian for your children and pets. Where minors are concerned, the courts will likely name your surviving spouse as guardian. And, without specific directions provided in your own personalized document, the guardian may have to petition the court for money simply to meet your children's needs.

ESTABLISHING TRUSTS

Consider also the establishment of trust funds for your children, your spouse, close friends, relatives, employees and others. A trust insures an income for beneficiaries of the trust and provides for emergency situations. You may wish to establish a trust for a charitable cause, or an organization as an expression of your philosophy, also.

You may stipulate in your will that taxes to be paid on your estate come "off the top" rather than from individual shares. With careful pre-planning these tax liabilities, too, can be greatly lessened.

OTHER CONSIDERATIONS

There is also the remote possibility of simultaneous deaths and alternative plans to cover this unlikely eventuality should be included in the will.

Once your will is written keep a copy in some place where it will not be lost or stolen. Keep it in a place where it can easily be found by the executor or friend. Place the original on file with your attorney. It is not a good idea to keep it in a safe deposit box.

Keep in mind that estate laws differ from state to state and you would be well advised to contact your own lawyer on specific bequests.

But regardless of your bequests, the very act of preparing a will means you have taken control of your own financial planning. This step can bring you tremendous rewards - not only to your own sense of self and value, but to generations far into the future. Your will becomes a document which attests to both your caring and your ability to share and be concerned.

SAMPLE OF A "WILL"

YOU SHOULD CONSULT AN ATTORNEY FOR THE PREPARATION OF YOUR WILL, MINDFUL THAT THIS IS MERELY A GUIDE AND SAMPLE COPY OF A WILL, WHICH MUST BE WITNESSED BY THREE INDIVIDUALS AND NOTARIZED. THE TESTATOR SHOULD SIGN THE BOTTOM OF EACH PAGE.

IN THE NAME OF GOD, AMEN.

I,   residing at

County of   State of   being of sound and disposing mind, memory and understanding, do hereby make, publish and declare this instrument as and to be my Last Will and Testament, hereby expressly revoking any and all other Wills or Codicils heretofore made by

me.

FIRST: I direct that the cost and expense of the administration of my Estate, all my debts, and the cost and expense of my last illness be first paid. I direct that all inheritance, transfer, succession, Estate and other such taxes or assessments levied against my Estate, or its inheritance by or transfer to any beneficiary, shall be paid out of my general Estate and not charged against any particular beneficiary, including insurance beneficiaries.

SECOND: I give and bequeath

to the following:

A.

B. ETC.....ETC.....

THIRD; I hereby give and bequeath to

ETC...,.ETC.....,.ETC.....

FOURTH: All the rest, residue and remainder of my Estate, consisting primarily of whether real, personal or mixed, wheresoever situate and of whatsoever the same may consist whereof I may die, seized or possessed or to which I may be entitled at the time of my death, I give, devise and bequeath as follows:

A.   (What   you   bequeath)   to

_____

residing at   to have and to hold for (his or her)

own use forever.

In the event (my daughter)   shall predecease me leaving issue her

surviving, I hereby order and direct that the share she would have received go to my daughter

_____IN TRUST NEVERTHELESS, for education, benefit, maintenance,

support and care of any of such issue until the youngest child shall reach the age of twenty-one (21)

years, at which time I order and direct that the trust shall terminate and the balance of the corpus

of the trust, together with any accumulations thereon be paid to the issue of my daughter,

, in equal shares, share and share alike.

In the event my daughter,   shall predecease me leaving no issue her

surviving, I hereby order and direct that the share she would have received be redivided among

her (brothers and sisters)

B. (What you Bequeath) thereof to my daughter,

residing, in   to have and to hold for her own use forever.

In the event my daughter,   shall predecease me leaving issue her

surviving, I hereby order and direct that the share she would have received go to my daughter

, IN TRUST NEVERTHELESS, for the education, benefit, maintenance, support and care of

any of such issue until the youngest child shall reach the age of twenty-one (21) years, at which time

I order and direct that the trust shall terminate and the balance of the corpus of the trust, together

with any accumulations thereon be paid to the issue of my daughter, in equal shares, share and

share alike.

In the event of my daughter,   shall predecease me leaving no

issue her surviving, I hereby order and direct that the share she would have received be

redivided among her brother and sisters.

C. ETC........... ETC.......

FIFTH: I hereby nominate, constitute and appoint my daughter, Executrix of this, my Last Will and Testament, giving unto her full power and authority to mortgage, rent, lease, sell and convey any and all the real estate of which I may die seized or possessed, and to give good and sufficient of conveyance therefore.

In the event my daughter, _____ shall predecease me,

renounce, or having qualified, cease to function for any reason, I hereby nominate, constitute and appoint my daughter, _____ alternate Executor, in her place and stead, giving unto her the same power and authority heretofore given said designated Executrix.

SIXTH: I hereby order and direct that my Executrix, Trustees or alternate, as the case may be, heretofore named in this Will, not be required to give bond or other security in this jurisdiction or any other jurisdiction wherein proceedings may be taken in connection with this, my Will.

SEVENTH: I grant unto my Executors and Trustees (including any substitute or successor personal representatives or trustees), the following powers in addition to those powers from time to time granted by law of the State _____ to Executors and Trustees of residents during the course of the administration of my Estate and the trusts created hereto, the same to be exercised in such manner as in their reasonable discretion they may deem advisable, and to be applicable to all property, real and personal at any time forming part of my Estate of such trust:

1. To retain, temporarily or permanently, any or all property owned by me at the time of my death in the form in which it then exists; acquire by purchase, exchange or otherwise, and retain, temporarily or permanently, any kind of realty or personalty, including stocks and unsecured obligations, undivided interests, interest in investment trusts, mutual funds, common trust funds, leases and property which is outside my domicile, all without being limited to investments authorized or deposit monies of my Estate (or of any trust hereby created) in any one or more savings or other banks (including the fiduciary) in any form of account whether or not interest bearing.

2. To sell, exchange or otherwise dispose of realty and personalty publicly or privately, wholly or partly, on credit or for any consideration including stocks, bonds or other

corporate obligations, grant options for the purchase, exchange or other disposition of any such property.

   3. To pay legacies, establish trusts and divide or distribute principal in kind or in money or partly in each or by way of undivided interest.

   4. In addition to any of the powers heretofore given to trustees, and in addition to paying over the net income for the benefit of the beneficiary, trustees are authorized in their sole and absolute discretion at any time and from time to time to pay or apply from the corpus of the trust (even to the point of completely exhausting same) such amounts as it may deem advisable to provide adequately and properly for the support, maintenance, welfare and comfort of the beneficiary of the trust herein established.

I, _____ , the Testator, sign my name to this instrument this

Day of _____ , (year), and being duly sworn, do hereby declare to the undersigned authority that I sign it as my free and voluntary act for the purposes therein expressed, and that I am eighteen (18) years of age or older, of sound mind and under no constraint or undue influence.

We, the witnesses, sign our names to this instrument and being duly sworn, do hereby declare to the undersigned authority that the Testator signs and executes this instrument as his Last Will and that he signs it willingly and that each of us, in the presence and hearing of the Testator, hereby signs this Will as witness to the Testator's signing, and that to the best of our knowledge, the Testator is eighteen (18) years of age or older, of sound mind and under no constraint or undue influence.

_____ residing at_____

_____ residing at_____

_____ residing at_____

STATE OF   )
) SS:
COUNTY OF   )
Subscribed, sworn to and acknowledged before me by
_____the Testator, and subscribed and sworn to, before me
by,_____by_____and_____,
witnesses, this   day   of_____,_____

                    _____

LIVING TRUST

What is a trust?

A trust is a legal entity that is established to hold assets for your benefit , or for the benefit of others determined by you. A trust is managed by one or more trustees who are legally responsible for ensuring that the trust operates according to your wishes.

One significant advantage of trusts is that beneficiaries are able to receive income from the trust but you maintain control over how funds are distributed. For example, if you gave your 18-year-old son a $10,000 gift, he could spend the money immediately as he sees fit. However, if you established a trust instead, you could specify in trust that the funds are to be released to your son over a set period of years or only for a specific purpose, such as college expenses.

Types of living trust

A living trust is established between living persons, for instance, between parent and child, or opposed to a trust that is established by your will. Living trusts can be funded with securities, other property of money available for investment.

There are two types of living trusts: a revocable trust and an irrevocable trust. With a revocable living trust, you retain control of your assets while you're alive. "Revocable" means you can change beneficiaries, modify the terms of the trust, and even terminate or revoke the trust and get back your property. You have the option of naming yourself as a trustee so that you can continue to manage your assets, or appointing someone else as the trust's administrator.

After you die, the property in the trust is distributed directly to the beneficiaries without going through probate. As a result, estate settlement costs are likely to be reduced and your beneficiaries will have quick access to the trust's funds. Keep in mind, however, that revocable trusts offer no federal estate tax advantage. Because you retain control over the trust, the assets in the trust are included in your estate for federal estate tax purposes and also may be subject to state death taxes.

As the name implies, an irrevocable trust cannot be changed, modified or revoked, regardless of how your personal financial circumstances might change. You also cannot name yourself as trustee. For giving up control, you get a tax benefit: Funds put in this type of trust not only help reduce your current taxable income, but also generally are not subject to estate taxes because the trust owns the assets.

Another type of irrevocable trust – an irrevocable life insurance trust – often appeals to those who substantial life insurance policies. The value of certain life insurance policies, which are normally included in your estate for tax purposes, can be excluded by creating this type of trust. However, there is a trade-off. When you transfer your insurance policies to the trust, you give up all ownership rights, the right to assign the policy to the trust, you give up all ownership rights, the right to assign the policy to anyone and the right to borrow against the policy's cash value. When you die, the trust is the beneficiary of the policy and the policy's value may be excluded from the estate for tax purposes.

Determining the need for living trusts

Before spending the time and money – generally, $1,000 to $3,000 – to set up a living trust, it's wise to discuss with CPA how the trust fits into your overall estate and financial plans. You'll want to consider whether or not you can afford to set aside funds in a trust permanently without changing your current life-style, and the extent to which you want to provide for your heirs and beneficiaries.

REMEMBERING YOUR HEIRS

Remember the old saying: taxes and death are inevitable? That may be so, but taxes on death are not. In 1997 Congress passed and the President signed a new tax loss which increases the $600,000 exemption for estate taxes. The tax exemption will be phased in as follows:

1998 -	$625,000
1999 -	650,000
2000 -	675,000
2001 -	700,000
2004 -	850,000
2005 -	950,000
2006 -	1,000,000

If all your assets amount to less than $625,000, you are home free. The Federal Government allows each person to leave that much to heirs without incurring taxes. A will dictating who gets what generally suffices as an estate plan.

But before you breathe a sigh of relief, take a close look at your financial picture. Many couples, even those who consider themselves solidly middle class, are over that threshold once they value their houses and other property. Pension plans and 401(k) savings are often overlooked, as are life insurance policies, whose payouts will be included in the estate.

Planning for death is not a pleasant task, but can reduce taxes and leave more of your estate intact for your heirs. Financial consultants cite other reasons for an estate plan. The best plans meet family goals: They ensure that adult children are not shortchanged by a stepparent or that a family business remains intact or that a favorite charity gets a final gift.

Just as people underestimate their assets, they underestimate estate taxes. Uncle Sam collects 37 cents to 60 cents on every dollar over $625,000. An efficient way to sidestep such taxes is to give away some assets. Each person can give up to $40,000 annually to as many people as desired without incurring gift taxes, so a couple can transfer $20,000 a year to each child and grandchild as a way to shrink an estate.

Experts particularly encourage shifting assets that are likely to appreciate in value. If, for instance, you have a successful business, consider giving your adult children and grandchildren a small stake every year in that business. Those who fear losing control of the business can defuse this landmine by keeping at least 50 percent of the assets. An added benefit to this strategy is financing your grandchildren's education.

Another way to skirt taxes is a bypass trust. Legal fees for drafting a couple's wills with the provisions for a bypass trust would be about $1,000 to $1,500, say estate-planning experts. A couple with over $625,000 in assets can avoid estate taxes when one of them dies by having wills that stipulate everything goes to the survivor. This is the so-called spouse exemption in estate taxes.

First, the couple should switch their assets from joint to individual ownership. If the husband dies first (and actuarial tables say he will), his portion of the assets can go into a bypass trust, with the children named as the eventual beneficiaries. His wife gets the income from the trust and can tap the principal for living expenses if needed. At her death, the trust assets go to the children, tax-free. As long as the wife's estate conforms to the graduated scale noted above, she can escape Federal Estate Taxes.

Estate planning can be especially challenging when parents have liquid assets such as a farm or a business. In many cases, adult children are forced to liquidate such assets because of estate taxes. To generate cash to pay estate taxes, you can create a trust for your children that holds a second-to-die life insurance policy. The policy, which pays out when the second partner dies, costs less than two individual life insurance policies. By putting it in a trust, the policy will be excluded from the estate and estate taxes.

Life insurance trusts can be even more efficient for passing money to grandchildren. In this way, one can shelter property from estate taxes for two generations.

Life insurance trusts are not simple, but they can be explained by a financial adviser and created by a lawyer. But the complexity of estate planning is not the main stumbling block to accomplishing the task. What is? The answer, according to most financial planners, is that no one wants to deal with the inevitability of death.

DEFINITIONS OF SOME HELPFUL LEGAL TERMS

Ancillary - An ANCILLARY executor is subordinate to the one named in your will and is appointed to dispose of property in another State or county which does not permit your chosen executor to represent you.

Codicil - A written instrument executed and witnessed like your will, to change or add to its provisions.

Custodian - A financial institution (or individual) with whom property is left to be taken care of under a letter of instructions.

Donor - One who creates a trust - also known as grantor or settlor.

Escrow - Cash, securities, important documents or other property are deposited with an agent to be delivered by the agent to a third party upon fulfillment of conditions prescribed in a letter of instruction.

Estate - Your ESTATE is all your own - real estate, cash, stocks, bonds, and other property. You can pass these on by will subject to the deduction of debts, estate and inheritance taxes and administration expenses.

Executor - Your EXECUTOR is named by you in your will to settle your estate and see that it is https://www.alladvantage.com/cashsecure.asppassed along as you direct in the will.

Fiduciary
Services - Those rendered by an executor or trustee or committee or guardian of property.

Insurance
Trust - A "living trust" in which the property trusted consists partly or entirely of the right to receive proceeds of life insurance policies.

Letters
Testamentary - The Court's certificate of the probate of a will and of the executor's authority to act under it.

Living Trust - While living you turn over money or other property to a trustee to manage during an agreed period, which may extend beyond your lifetime.

Minor - A child under legal age; legal age differs in different states.

Principal - The PRINCIPAL or CORPUS of an estate or trust is the property in it other than income.

Probating
a Will - Presenting proof to the Court after your death of the legality of your Last Will and Testament, whereupon the Court grants authority to the executor to carry out your intentions expressed in the will.

Remainderman -	One who is entitled to share in the principal of a trust fund when the trust terminates and the principal is finally distributed.
Surrogate -	The judge of a probate or surrogate's court, having jurisdiction over wills, executors and testamentary trustees.
Testamentary Trust -	A TESTAMENTARY TRUST is one created by a will to become effective after.
Testator -	One who has made a will.
Trust -	A TRUST puts your money or other property into the hands of a trustee for management, disposition of income and distribution of principal as you direct in your will or trust agreement.
Trustee -	The financial institution or individual (or both), named to manage and distribute, after your death, the income and principal of the trust funds as your will prescribes. This is a testamentary trustee. You may also appoint a trustee to manage property placed in a trust during your lifetime - a "living trust".
Will -	Your LAST WILL AND TESTAMENT contains your written direction s for disposal of your estate after your death.

SOURCES OF INFORMATION

There follows a list of source material with information as to how the materials may be obtained.

Survivors' Benefits- U.S. Government

Number	Title
CSCBRI 46-171	Information for Annuitants
CSCBRI 46-301	Information for Survivor Annuitants
CSCBRI 41-118	Information for Annuitants About Federal Employees Health Benefits
CSCBRI 46-214-E	Annuity Benefits Under the Civil Service Retirement System

The above publications are available from the Office of Personnel Management, Retirement and Insurance Program, 1900 E Street, N.W., Washington D.C. 20415.

Social Security

Number	Title
DHEW(SSA)1440	Rights and Responsibilities for Those Who Receive Social Security Retirement or Survivor Benefits
DHEW(SSA)10035	Your Social Security
DHEW(SSA)10037	What Your Medical Insurance Pays
DHEW(SSA)10050	Your Medicare Handbook
DHEW(SSA)78-10388	Recent Changes in Social Security

The above publications are available through offices of the Social Security Administration in your area.

Veterans' Benefits

Number	Title
IS-1 Fact Sheet	Federal Benefits for Veterans and Dependents Veterans Administration.

This publication is available at the Veterans Administration Regional Office in your area.

Taxes

Number	Title
IRS Publication 524	Tax Credit for the Elderly
IRS Publication 567	Tax Information on Civil Service Retirement and Disability
IRS Publication 575	Tax Information on Pensions and Annuity Income

These publications may be obtained from State or Regional Offices of the Internal Revenue Service. Note: Number and title of source material subject to revision.

MISCELLANEOUS

ADDITIONAL IMPORTANT INFORMATION

MISCELLANEOUS

ADDITIONAL IMPORTANT INFORMATION

_____
_____
_____
_____
_____
_____
_____
_____
_____
_____
_____
_____
_____
_____
_____
_____
_____
_____
_____
_____
_____
_____
_____
_____
_____
_____
_____
_____

FAREWELL
MY DEARLY BELOVED

I have always loved you more than words can ever say,
remember how we whispered our love for each other everyday.

We always laughed and danced and tried so hard to sing
for all this joy, you were truly the wind beneath my wings.

May all of our memories remain in your heart and eyes
for I shall wait for you in the "Lord's Paradise".

All of my fondest Love,

ACKNOWLEDGMENTS

1. Pascack Valley Community Life Newspaper, Westwood, NJ, for the use of an article concerning "Living Trusts", which appeared in the October 23, 1996 issue.

2. Seniority Magazine, for use of an article concerning "Heirs", which appeared in the August 1995 issue.

3. United States Office of Personnel Management (OPM), for use of their information pertaining to "Retired Federal Workers".

4. Social Security Administration, for use of general information pertaining to benefits for individuals.

5. State of N.J. Police & Firemens Retirement System Handbook from which general instructional data was utilized for the assistance of "Retired State Civil Service Employees" including Police and Firemen.

6. Society of Former FBI Agents - Retirement Handbook from which general instructional data was utilized with permission.

ABOUT THE
AUTHOR

Albert F. Chestone was born in Waterbury, Connecticut. He earned his BS Degree at Ohio University, Athens, Ohio, and received his Masters Degree from New York University. He is a veteran of WWII having served with the Air Force in Africa and Italy. His first wife, Marcie Chestone, who also graduated from Ohio University, died in Jan 1980. They had five Children. Al served as a Special Agent of the FBI for almost 30 years. He is president of Supreme Associates, an Executive Recruiting firm specializing in placing Security Directors into the corporate environment. Al is currently married to a former widow, Lorraine Ryan, mother of four. They reside in NJ. Al is a member of Phi Delta Theta Fraternity, Society of Former FBI Agents; American Society for Industrial Security; Federal Law Enforcement Officers Association and the Bergen County Police Chief's Association, State of NJ.

*Appreciation is expressed to
Mrs. Kathryn K. (Panzironi) Spooner,
Former President of, KAYE KANE ENTERPRISES, INC.,
Ridgewood, N.J., and Denis McKeown of Manhasset, L.I., NY
for their assistance in the preparation of this publication.

www.ingramcontent.com/pod-product-compliance
Lightning Source LLC
Chambersburg PA
CBHW080419290526
45791CB00008BA/2335